The Library of Living and Working in Colonial Times™

A Day in the Life of a Colonial Cabinetmaker

Amy French Merrill

The Rosen Publishing Group's

For my brothers

Published in 2002 by The Rosen Publishing Group, Inc.
29 East 21st Street, New York, NY 10010

First Edition

Book Design: Danielle Primiceri
Layout Design: Maria E. Melendez and Nick Sciacca
Project Editor: Frances E. Ruffin

Photo Credits: Title page, p. 19 © North Wind Pictures; pp. 4, 7 © Historical Picture Archive/CORBIS; p. 8 © CORBIS; p. 11 © The Granger Collection; p. 12 © Philadelphia Museum of Art/CORBIS; pp. 15, 16 © Peter Harholdt/CORBIS; p. 20 © Bettman/CORBIS.

Merrill, Amy French.
A day in the life of a colonial cabinetmaker / Amy French Merrill.
    p. cm. — (The library of living and working in colonial times)
ISBN 8239-5822-1
1. Cabinetwork—United States—History—18th century—Juvenile literature. 2. Cabinetmakers—United States—History—18th century—Juvenile literature. [1. Cabinetwork. 2. Cabinetmakers. 3. United States—History—Colonial period, ca. 1600–1775.] I. Title. II. Series.
TT197 .M45 2002
684.1'04'097409032—dc21

                                                                00–013015

Manufactured in the United States of America

Contents

1   A Master Craftsman   5

2   Apprentices and Journeymen   6

3   Working with Wood   9

4   Tools of the Craft   10

5   Made to Order   13

6   Furniture Design   14

7   From Start to Finish   17

8   The Importance of Joints   18

9   Current Events   21

10 Closing Time   22

    Glossary   23

    Index   24

    Web Sites   24

Plan

Feet

A Master Craftsman

On a fall morning in 1763, William Smith walked through the woodshed that connected his home and his shop. Several workers were already there, busily preparing for the day. William was a cabinetmaker. He made furniture and other items from wood. William lived in Newport, a city in the **colony** of Rhode Island. People throughout the colonies knew of the fine work done by cabinetmakers there. William was a **master craftsman**. His shop was known for producing some of the most beautiful furniture in the colonies.

◀ *These pieces of furniture are examples of items that may have been made during colonial times.*

Apprentices and Journeymen

William Smith's fine furniture brought many customers to his shop. To help him, William had taken on a young **apprentice** named Daniel. As an apprentice, Daniel did not receive any pay, but William taught him mathematics, how to read and write, and all of the skills he would need to become a master cabinetmaker. William also hired a few journeymen who were paid to work in his shop. Journeymen were skilled workers who had completed their time as apprentices but were not yet master craftsmen.

This is a drawing of men working ▶
in a cabinetmaker's shop.

Working with Wood

When William Smith made a piece of furniture, he first chose the type of wood he would use. Like other **colonial** cabinetmakers, he used many different types of wood. William's favorite wood was mahogany. Mahogany was **imported** from the West Indies, a group of islands off the southeast coast of North America. The colonies sent items such as flour and meat to be sold in the West Indies and received wood and sugar in return. Sometimes a piece of furniture was made of more than one type of wood.

◀ *Cabinetmakers used woods from trees found in the colonies, such as cherry, maple, oak, chestnut, walnut, and pine.*

Tools of the Craft

A colonial cabinetmaker made each piece of furniture by hand. He used many different tools to shape raw wood into fine furniture. William's shop had many kinds of saws and hammers. He used drills to make holes in the wood. Scrapers, knives, and **chisels** shaped the wood. William used metal files to make the wood's surface perfectly smooth. One very important tool was the lathe. A lathe was a machine used to hold and rotate wood. As the lathe turned, the cabinetmaker guided the wood along a cutting tool to shape it.

In this cabinetmaker's workroom, apprentices turned the wheel of a very large lathe to shape a piece of furniture. ▶

Made to Order

By midmorning everyone in the shop took a break. They gathered for some cornbread and apple cider. Then a customer entered the shop. The man was John Stuart, a neighbor. As William invited him to share the food, John told William he wanted a new table on which to serve tea. The table was a special gift for his daughter, who was getting married. A cabinetmaker made all kinds of furniture, including chairs, chests, beds, and desks. He also put finishing touches, such as **molding** and window frames, on a new home.

◄ *These colonial chests, known as highboys and lowboys, are on exhibit at the Philadelphia Museum of Art.*

Furniture Design

Much of the furniture built in William's shop was made in the style of a famous English cabinetmaker named Thomas Chippendale. Furniture made in this style had beautiful designs carved into the wood. The legs and feet often were made in the shapes of animals' claws. The Goddard and Townsend families were Rhode Island **Quakers** who practiced the trade of cabinetmaking. A desk made by the Goddards or Townsends might be decorated with wood carved in the shapes of shells.

This chair was made in the Chippendale style. Furniture made by the Goddards and Townsends ▶ was considered the best of all colonial cabinetwork.

From Start to Finish

Once William selected the wood he wanted to use for a piece of furniture, each part of the design was cut separately. Next the individual parts were shaped carefully. Then all of the parts were joined to make the final product. A cabinetmaker always put a **finish** on his furniture. Sometimes William instructed Daniel to rub coat after coat of oil into the wood. Daniel rubbed until he could see his reflection in the surface of the wood. For other pieces of furniture, William applied a kind of paint called a stain.

◀ *This is a Chippendale-style chest of drawers made by an American cabinetmaker.*

The Importance of Joints

One of the most difficult and important steps in making a piece of furniture was joining its parts. An experienced cabinetmaker took great care in creating joints. These were the points at which the pieces of wood were fitted together. A piece of furniture with poorly made joints could be unsteady or could fall apart completely! William took great pride in making perfect joints, and he worked hard to teach Daniel this necessary skill.

Cabinetmakers relied on the strength of the joints they made to hold furniture together. Nails or screws never were used by a master craftsman. ▶

Current Events

In the afternoons, William often asked Daniel to read the newspaper out loud for the shop workers. Much of the news in recent months had included reports about the **French and Indian War**. The French and English originally had settled in different areas of North America. When both France and England wanted to expand their territories to the west, a war broke out. Native Americans fought on the side of the French. That day's paper had wonderful news for the English colonists. The war was over!

◀ *This is a drawing of a battle fought during the French and Indian War.*

Closing Time

At the end of the day, the workers cleaned the shop while William looked over a list of orders from his customers. He recorded the day's work, checked his supply of wood, and planned for the tasks to be completed the next afternoon. At home, William's wife, Meg, had a large pot of stew waiting for him and the apprentice Daniel. During dinner, William and Meg discussed the events of the day. After eating a dessert of pear tart, Daniel completed chores and William relaxed by the fire. Next door, the cabinet shop was quiet, at least until morning.

Glossary

apprentice (uh-PREN-tis) A young person learning a skill or trade.

chisels (CHIH-zulz) Tools with sharp edges used to cut and shape wood.

colonial (kuh-LOH-nee-ul) Having to do with the period of time when the United States was made of 13 colonies ruled by England.

colony (KAH-luh-nee) An area in a new country where a large group of people move, who are still ruled by the leaders and laws of their old country.

finish (FIH-nish) A final coating for the surface of wood.

French and Indian War (FRENCH AND IN-dee-un WOR) The battles fought between 1754 and 1763 by England, France, and Native American allies for control of North America.

imported (im-PORT-id) Brought in from a foreign country for sale or use.

master craftsman (MAS-tur KRAFS-mun) An established worker with special skills.

molding (MOHLD-ing) A strip of wood used to decorate the wall of a room, a door, or a piece of furniture.

Quakers (KWAY-kurz) People who belong to a religion that believes in peace and equality for all people.

Index

A
apprentice, 6, 22

C
Chippendale,
    Thomas, 14

F
French and Indian
    War, 21

G
Goddard family,
    14

J
joints, 18
journeymen, 6

N
Newport, Rhode
    Island, 5

Q
Quakers, 14

S
stain, 17

T
tools, 10
Townsend family,
    14

W
West Indies, 9
wood, 5, 9, 10,
    17, 18

Web Sites

To learn more about colonial cabinetmakers, check out
these Web sites:
www.history.org/life/trades/tradecab.htm
www.kidinfo.com/American_History/Colonization_
Colonial_Life.html